99 & Still Counting

Ginny Nickoloff

All rights reserved. No part of this book may be used or reproduced in any manner whatsoever without written permission except in the case of brief quotations embodied in crucial articles and reviews.

Copyright © 2024 by Virginia Nickoloff

ISBN 13: 978-1-951543-28-0

DANCING CROWS
PRESS

Also by Ginny Nickoloff

Grossly Outnumbered!

My Platinum Years

Very Truly Yours (coming 2024)

Children's books:

Granny with the Freckled Knees:
    Book One—Africa
    Book Two---Africa
    Book Three--Thailand
    Book Four—Egypt

A Tale of Two Tails (coming 2024)

Dedication:

For my children and grandchildren
and anyone who wonders
about the Greatest Generation.

Table of Contents

Chapter		Page
1	Ginny	1
2	Parties	10
3	Telephone	13
4	Sleepwalking, Circus and Names	17
5	Earthquakes	21
6	Racial Discrimination	25
7	Dancing, Singing and Reading	28
8	Tanlova	31
9	Pets	41
10	Movies	44
11	Radio	53
12	Television	56
13	Ballroom Dancing	59
14	Fashion	65
15	Hairstyles and Makeup	74
16	Automobiles	82
17	Airplanes	92
18	Space	96
19	Smartphone and AI	99
20	Shopping	101
21	Grocery shopping	108

22	Appliances	111
23	Games	119
24	Computers	124
25	Sports	126
26	Astrology and Travel	130
27	Jokes	134
28	Health	137
29	Women	140
30	Finale	142

Chapter 1

Ginny

I was born in 1924, the last year of the Greatest Generation, (1901-1924) and before the Silent Generation (1925-1945). I will speak up while my memory can still recall what happened in those early years not to mention yesterday.

Nine months old   Santa Ana, CA

Five years old
Long Beach, California

Eleven years old
Audubon Junior High School
Los Angeles, California

Sixteen years old
Manual Arts High School graduation
Los Angeles, California

Ninety-eighth birthday
Villa Rica, Georgia

My scarf is a gift son Jim brought from Australia.

Speaking of yesterday, my 99th birthday

    My house was full of people, twenty plus my two cats and granddaughter Mary's Labradoodle. I counted twelve people in my kitchen at one time. All the beds were full plus sleeping bags on the floor for two nights.

Granddaughter Mary's little daughter, Natalie (age 6) and granddaughter Lauren's daughter Clementine (age 4) paraded around in princess dresses.

They all had fun playing in the lake.

Clementine   Natalie   Avery

Going back to my early years, my mother was a talented seamstress, and I often spent my day sitting on the floor next to her sewing machine while she taught me the alphabet and reading Dick and Jane.

My memory really kicked in at five years old when I picked all the carnations in our neighbor's front yard. My mother pulled a switch off a forsythia bush and whipped my legs. That wasn't the only time I received that punishment.

I learned early on that "Mother knows best!" She didn't like me to go barefooted but finally gave in. The first thing I did was to take a spade and start to dig a hole in the hard dirt. The first plunge of the spade missed the dirt and hit my big toe. Blood everywhere! Mom picked me up and sat me on the kitchen counter with my foot in the sink and ran it full of water turning it blood red! A week or so later, while playing in the sprinklers in the front yard, my toenail floated off. Happily, it grew back in.

Mom raised chickens in our backyard in Santa Ana, California. Getting chicken dinner ready entailed killing the chicken first. We had a big stump in the backyard. She would catch the chicken and lay its head on the stump and chop it off! The body of the chicken would run around the yard a few times before dropping dead. You don't forget that image! Mom would sit on the back porch steps and pluck the feathers out.

Chapter 2

Parties

More pleasant memories involved parties at our house. Some were bridge parties; some were lacy handkerchief parties. Everyone would bring a pretty new handkerchief and there would be an exchange. That definitely would not happen today. How long since you carried a handkerchief? The invention of Kleenex put a stop to that!

Some were just parties where the guests gathered around the piano and sang songs. My friend, Barbara, and I would tap dance to "On the Sidewalks of New York." Remember "East Side, West Side, all around the town"?

I was crazy about olives and, one party night at our house, Mom had the bowl of olives ready to serve in the kitchen. Fool that I was, I ate the whole bowl before the guests arrived. Mom was not happy!

San Gabriel Court was a fun neighborhood. Someone was always giving a party. The Andersons who lived three doors down, had a white elephant party one year. I wrapped up an old electric heater covered with cobwebs that was stored in our garage. The Danowsky's brought a great big TV antenna they didn't use anymore. (Remember when you couldn't get TV reception without an antenna?)

The next year, I came home and saw a fancy package on the front steps. My neighbor who had picked my white elephant package, had sprayed the heater gold, cobwebs and all, and wrapped it in Christmas paper.

We had a really big party when Jimmy passed the California bar exam. We were new in the neighborhood, and he hadn't told anyone that he had taken the exam. He was waiting out in the front yard for the mailman. When the mailman came with a big package for him, he knew he had passed.

To celebrate, I invited everyone on the street and even a few from around the corner so that no one would complain to the police department. We set up a pool table in one bedroom, a card table with puzzle pieces in another bedroom, a croquet set in the backyard (before we had the pool). I bought all the macaroni they had at Robert's Market and served a midnight supper. The party went on until 5 a.m. but, pregnant with Jac, I went across the street and went to bed at the Poolman's house with Rosemary about 3 a.m.

Chapter 3

Telephone

When I was three years old, the first telephone call was made between the United States and England. Visiting my Auntie Blanche in Minnesota when I was four years old, she had a "party line". If the call was for her, it had three rings. When her phone rang only once, she told me to pick it up and listen in on the conversation. I couldn't believe she wanted me to do that. There was no privacy in those days.

My mom worked her small-town Salem, South Dakota's telephone switchboard when she was a teenager. She was dating my dad and when another girl would call him, she would pull the plug (disconnect).

The first phone I saw was a big thing on the wall of my grandfather's house in South Dakota. We got our first phone in Long Beach. It was a small one on the wall in our breakfast room with a dial to dial the number. Later telephones sat on a table and hung up in a cradle. They also had a dial, and you dialed the number.

We had a rotary phone with a dial on it. It wasn't until we moved to Georgia in 1992 that we had a wireless phone we could walk around with even though we had one in the bedroom, TV room and our office. It identified the caller and also took messages if I didn't answer the phone. You could block a number which I did all the time when the caller ID is "unavailable". These are advertisers that drive me nuts.

My message when I don't answer is "This is Ginny. Call me back unless you are trying to sell me something."

Telephone numbers used to have prefixes depending on where you lived. Ours in Sierra Madre was ELgin so you would dial an E and L before you dialed the number. My mom's number was AXminister and my mother-in-law's was WEbster. This was because the telephone company didn't think people could remember so many numbers.

Now addresses have zip codes for physical location and area codes for telephone locations. All speeding up the delivery system.

Long distance calls were expensive when we lived in Sierra Madre. Our small-town borders (two miles long and one mile wide), were the only place we could call without extra-long-distance charges. The only other place we could call without extra charges was Mount Wilson, thousands of feet above us. We didn't know a soul up there. Nowadays, I can call anywhere in the United States for very little.

When I worked for the lawyers in Los Angeles, I operated a small switchboard so I could transfer calls to the five lawyers or their secretaries. I would answer "Boyle, Holmes, Frye, Garrett, and Cheesebrough. How may I help you."

One day, Mr. Garrett was having a big meeting in our conference room. He called me in and told me to call the airlines and get him a flight to San Francisco that afternoon. When I called, the airlines told me they had no empty seats. With this information, my boss yelled at me and said I had to get him a seat. I was so mad, I said, "What do you want me to do—build you a seat?" and I stormed out of the room. Later, he apologized.

When I call the phone company for help with my television, I'm often talking to someone in the Philippines or India. The same when I need help with the computer.

I refuse to get a cell phone or the newest invention called a smartphone. I see everyone with a smartphone in hand almost all the time. It is like an appendage. They can't be without it. Granted, it can do almost everything including taking pictures and send them to friends. It is like having a computer in your hand. I spend enough time in front of my computer, I don't need to carry one with me.

I can conceive in the future that we will be just a head with a finger sticking out of the top. I guess with just a head, we can still see and kiss each other. Is that what we want?

Chapter 4

Sleepwalking, Circus, and Names

Sleepwalking in my early years had some interesting results. One time I put another pair of pajamas over the ones I had on. When I was about 12, I got up from my bed and went into the living room and fell asleep on the couch. This was all possible because sleeping is my best accomplishment to this day. I have always been able to take a short nap by visualizing the hands of a clock advancing 15 minutes or whatever time I wanted to wake up.

In Los Angeles, we lived six blocks from the Carlton Theater. Daddy drove us to the theater and on the way home I fell asleep in the back seat. My folks went in the house and Daddy said, "Where is Virginia?" I was asleep in the backseat of the car. Not surprising since, in later years, I could sleep standing up hanging on the strap on the streetcar on my way home from work and wake up when the conductor called my street.

A strong early memory reminds me of waiting on the curb with my classmates in first grade for the circus to pass by. It set up its tents not too far away. My dad took me to see the elephants and all the animals and bought me a chocolate ice cream cone which I managed to spill down my new red coat Mom had made for me. Dad got a bawling out, not me!

I lived long enough to see the demise of the Barnum and Bailey Circus. That was a sad day. Truly, there has been nothing to replace its acrobatic performers on the high bars under the big tent, decorated elephants with pretty girls riding on them, men in a cage challenging lions, and barkers inviting people into tents to see all manner of strange people or things. For a few cents, you could throw balls or shoot at passing ducks for prizes. The circus traveled the country bringing all this excitement right to the edge of your town.

We lived on the outer edge of Santa Ana, California, in a new subdivision until I was six. My friend, Barbara Loughboro, lived next door and Anna DeGroot lived down the street (Orange Avenue). These two friends remained best friends until they passed away even though we seldom lived in the same town or even state.

It is funny how names can affect one. First of all, I didn't like the name Virginia Lee or my last name Schmidt. Schmidt because I was teased that it rhymed with shit. Even worse, my mom's maiden name was Lola Virginia Schmidt so when she married my dad, Clarence William Schmidt, she didn't change her last name.

In business, my dad used C.W. as his first name, but he was known by all his family and friends as Tanny because the little kids in his family couldn't say Clarence. And so, he was Grandpa Tanny to my kids.

And there were four Virginia Lee's in my 10th grade Social Studies class. Our teacher gave us each a number.

I think I became Ginny by the time I was in high school and later, I was happy to be Nickoloff instead of Schmidt.

Nickoloff is Macedonian. When my father-in-law came to this country, he spelled it Nickoloff and when his brother came, he spelled it Nickloff without the o in the middle. My friend, Marlyn, who married Jimmy's cousin Art was Nickloff. She was adamant that her married last name was Nickloff, not Nickoloff.

My son Tom recently decided to pronounce his last name with the accent on the middle "o". Nick-O-loff. Even more interesting is that son Jac's daughter, Lauren, legally changed her middle name from Ann to Nickoloff. Her married name is Lauren Nickoloff Mcfall.

Chapter 5

Earthquakes

It is funny how one can remember odd names. My fourth-grade nature study class teacher was Mrs. Dudenbostle. Around the top of the cupboards in her class, she had put bird nests and other interesting things. I doubt there is even a nature study class anymore.

Fremont Elementary School in Long Beach had a new auditorium with a beautiful crystal chandelier. In 1933, I was eight years old in the fourth grade when the big earthquake (6.9 on the Richter scale) hit Long Beach. I wasn't happy until I found out that the chandelier was okay even though the whole school had to be demolished.

Once school was resumed, months later, our classes were in the front yard of the school under beach umbrellas. We had to bring our lunch and water in a Mason jar every day. (No plastic bottles of water in my day). In case you don't know what a Mason jar is, it is the jar that both my mom and, now, my granddaughter Mary preserve fruit and vegetables.

My life could have ended at 8 years old. That fateful day, I had walked from my elementary school to Jefferson Junior High to see the play *Little Women*. I walked home after the play and was sitting at the kitchen table telling my mom about the play while she was stirring something on the stove.

When the quake hit, she could see I was paralyzed with fear. She grabbed me and pulled me around the kitchen table as everything was crashing down out of the cupboards. Our built-in icebox came out of the wall in front of us, blocking our way to get around the table and then with another shake, it went back into the wall and Mom pulled me out to the back porch. We were thrown down the four or five steps and landed face down on the driveway. Mom's watch broke as her wrist slammed on the pavement.

She left me hanging onto the grass in the front yard while she turned off our gas meter and then checked our neighbors' gas meters.

When she came back to me, I was crying and worried about my first doll with real hair, Mary Ann. Mom ran in the house between quakes and reported back that Mary Ann was all right. I soon learned what a pillar of strength my mom was.

The play had ended, and only the janitor was killed when the quake hit, and the roof crashed on the seats. If the quake had hit an hour earlier, I would have been under that roof and not here telling my story.

The radio was warning people who lived by the ocean that there was a possibility of a tidal wave and advised them to go to high ground. We lived on a hill, so our beach friends came to our house and camped in our back yard. My mom built a fire pit out of fallen bricks from a nearby church, big enough to heat a large laundry tub full of water to sterilize it for drinking and then she cooked on it for all these people. (I always said, "My mom could have crossed the prairies in a covered wagon with ten children and she would have had no problem.")

The first night we three slept in our car parked on the street as it shook and quaked all night long ... and then quaked for the next six months.

Mom cleaned up five bushel baskets of broken dishes and stuff in the kitchen. From that time on my mom tied kitchen cupboards together until she moved to Georgia.

I tied a tall curio cabinet to the wall in Apple Valley where we had a few earthquakes also. I had completely remodeled that house and I asked my builder where was the safest part in a quake and he said, "In the old part, Virginia." The old part was brick with rebar between the walls. Rebar was put into the Long Beach building code after the 1933 earthquake.

Earthquakes continued to terrorize me until I moved from California to Georgia. I did feel one here in Georgia in the middle of the night, just a rattle as my headboard hit the wall. I doubt anyone else felt it ... I'm just sensitive.

Chapter 6

Racial Discrimination

My folks felt sorry for me because I was so spooked as tremors kept coming long after the big quake. They took me to my Uncle Tony and Aunt Ella's house in Azusa because the tremors couldn't be felt there.

My uncle had a shoe store in the town and had a black man come to work every day to shine shoes. My uncle told me that this man had to leave early every day because he lived in Glendale and black people could not be seen on the streets after sundown in that town.

Thinking about that, I checked Google and sure enough, this is what I found:

> "On October 24, 2020, Glendale has become the first city in California and the third one in the nation to pass a resolution apologizing for its history as a "Sundown" town."

It is hard for me to believe that it took all those years before that wrong was righted. I'm glad that my grandchildren will never know how prejudiced people were in my day.

I am ashamed to tell how it was when I was young. All over our country, there were laws that kept people of color, Jews, and Orientals, from living in many areas. In Los Angeles there were areas where black people, Oriental people and Jewish people could not rent or buy property. When my Japanese friend, Shiku, and her husband, Tom, moved to Boston, they were surprised that there were no restrictions on Japanese, only Jewish and black. I'm guessing it was probably because there hadn't been any Japanese there before.

One of my friends in elementary school was Mary Anne Rolf. Since we were studying early American history, she insisted that she was part Indian and a descendant of Pocahontas who married John Rolf. She probably had as much right as congress woman Elizabeth Warren who claims Indian heritage.

People did tend to live with their own kind, since we were all immigrants after 1492. My Greek friend, Betty Argy, was from Chicago, and she told me that her aunt had lived in Chicago for 25 years and never spoke

English because she lived in an area settled by Greeks.

I loved going to a high school in Los Angeles whose district encompassed many of these segregated communities. I had Jewish, Mexican and Japanese friends. When the war broke out in my last year in high school, I was horrified when my Japanese friends were put into internment camps for the duration. Luckily, one of my best friends, Shiku Sameshima, was rescued by her church and sent to a college in the Midwest. One of my Jewish friends and her father had just escaped from Nazi Germany.

My stalwart mom was the block warden during World War II. She was responsible for our very large block. Whenever there was a warning siren, she would circle the whole block checking to make sure that the people had filled their bathtubs with water. She was also checking to see that all blinds were down and no lights showing. It was so eerie hearing the street cars go by our house at night in the dark.

My mother-in-law was ecstatic when the war ended, and the lights came back on. That Christmas, she had colored lights practically covering the bushes on the front of her house.

Chapter 7

Dancing, Singing, and Reading

In the sixth grade, a new girl came to class from New York City. She had taken dancing lessons and decided to teach about six of us girls how to tap dance. The first thing she taught me was how to do a backbend. We would meet at the band shell in Recreation Park. She brought a phonograph to accompany our dancing. After weeks of lessons, our families were invited to see our "production".

Now my six-year-old granddaughter, Natalie, is receiving instruction in ballet dancing, and, to my delight, I have attended two of her programs.

My mom sang in a big choral group conducted by Mr. Alfred during our years in Long Beach. I was also in a children's singing group. At Christmas time, 500 singers, including Mom and me, sang the Halleluiah Chorus on the steps outside of the big civic auditorium on Rainbow Pier. Mr. Alfred threatened us with death if anyone sang an extra

"Halleluiah". I was scared to sing more than the first few halleluiahs.

My mother had a much better education in a small town in South Dakota than I did. She was an avid reader, often reading after midnight. I guess because she read so much, I didn't want to read at all. I am ashamed to admit that I would do a book report for school just by reading the flap on the cover. It was my loss!

Finally, in the ninth grade, I read a history of President Johnson and found it fascinating. That was the start of my reading books from cover to cover. In fact, the longer a book, the more I wanted to read it.

Long Beach was experimenting with something called "progressive" education. Even worse, they would even-out class numbers by skipping students. I was put ahead twice so I graduated from high school at sixteen. Luckily, I had one teacher in the ninth grade who taught us how to diagram a sentence.

My childhood dream was to be a secretary to a Big Man and fly with him all over the world, taking dictation! Hence, in high school I majored in secretarial subjects: typing, shorthand, book-keeping.

Asking my mom how to spell something was fruitless. The same with the meaning of a word.

Her only answer was, "Look it up in the dictionary!" Every household had a set of encyclopedias and a dictionary. Nowadays, the smart phone, Google or my Alexa answers everything. Will we know more or less??? Will my mind forget to remember anything for more than five minutes as the information is always at my voice request. I don't have to remember. But could Alexa or a cell phone retain the memories I've been writing about?

Chapter 8

Tanlova

My Mom's best friends in her choral group decided to take the kids to camp for a week at Lake Arrowhead in the summer. The husbands would come for the weekend. These men nearly went nuts because the women's names were Lela, Lila, Lola and Laura. In desperation, they would just point and say "Lela, Lila, Lola, Laura!"

So crazy about the mountains, my folks purchased a 99-year lease on Lot #47 in the San Bernardino Mountains, about 100 miles and a three-hour drive from our house in Long Beach.

The man across the street was a carpenter and he and my folks would drive up every weekend with a load of lumber. This was 1935 and I was eleven years old.

The lot was located on a fast-running stream about six feet across. Called the Santa Ana River, it emptied into the ocean in Long Beach. There was no electricity or running water and the cold stream was our drinking water and icebox. Dad used a big milk can to bring water up to the house. It was amazing how Mom could make Jello by setting it surrounded by rocks in the water on the edge of the stream. She cooked on a big old woodstove, and you cannot believe how wonderful when the scent of bacon floated up to my bed upstairs in the morning.

My mom's idea was to build the fireplace in the middle of the house instead of the usual end. The main floor was the living room, dining room, kitchen, master bedroom and toilet, but while building, we built an outdoor "privy" with a Sears catalogue for toilet paper. (Actually, the catalogue was just for looks, imitating the old days.) The upstairs was one big room with five double beds in it.

And this brings to mind the many months we had a framework set up in our living room in Long Beach to make patchwork quilts for these five beds. The neighbor ladies all pitched in and sewed squares of material until there were enough quilts for all the beds.

When Mom sold the cabin years later, I asked her if she kept the quilts and to my chagrin, she said no. I'm sorry that my boys never stayed at the cabin where my childhood through high school hinged. We played horseshoe and walked down the stream a ways to a Y.M.C.A. camp in the evenings and joined them singing around their fire.

There was a lake for fishing about four miles away, but Daddy caught fish in the stream right in front of our cabin. Hiking up the mountain behind our cabin was always an adventure and, in the winter, we could slide down the mountain in the snow.

My senior year in high school, we invited my leadership class, including the practice teacher, Howie Snyder, to spend a weekend at our cabin Tanlova. Tan for my dad, Tanny, lo for my mom, Lola, and va for Virginia. The boys slept in the cabin next door and the girls slept in Tanlova.

Saturday night, after dark, we gathered around our living room fireplace with the fire down to just hot coals giving off an eerie glow. Our teacher told a ghost story and we girls all screamed!

Since Mom made pancakes on the wood stove, she had the boys chopping wood. It was probably the only time in their lives, they ever chopped wood!

In the morning my dad challenged the boys to a pushup contest. Dad started with 100 pushups and none of the boys could outdo him. My dad did 100 pushups every morning before breakfast at home.

Daddy also had a ritual at breakfast. He made a list of ten things every New Year's Day that he wanted to accomplish in that year. One of the things on that list was a new Chevrolet and another thing listed was "the respect of his neighbors." At the end of the year, Daddy said he had accomplished everything on his list. When I asked him about the respect of his neighbors, he said he had gained their respect when they asked him who to vote for governor. They were Democrats and he was a Republican. And he bought the new Chevrolet for $600.

Mom kept a logbook for all our guests to sign. I still have that book and, reading all those names of our friends thanking us for a wonderful time and realizing I'm probably the only one still alive, is pretty overwhelming. My sons really got a kick out of some of the writings in this book.

Hearing the news last night, California is being hit by Hurricane Hilary with flooding not seen since 1939. And believe me, I do remember the flood of 1939. Because of the pouring rain, the little stream in front of our cabin became six feet deep and eight feet wide and changed direction between our cabin and the neighbor's cabin.

Our little stream was the beginning of the Santa Ana River which was usually dry as a bone as it ran to the Long Beach harbor. In that flood, the bridge between Long Beach and San Pedro was destroyed as this body of water rushed to the ocean.

Another really memorable weekend at Tanlova was October 16, 1943. So memorable that my mom wrote 4 pages in the book describing "one catastrophe after another." The war was in full force and tires were impossible to get. Not only tires, but coffee, sugar, and shoes required coupons issued to each person to obtain. My poor dad gave up his shoe coupons to me for four years.

I had a boyfriend, Harrison Packard, at the time who was in Naval officers' training at a college in Redlands. They were playing football Saturday afternoon and the plan was for we girls to go to the game and then all of us would go up to our cabin for the weekend. My mom was chaperone. The catastrophes my mom described involved the seven flat tires we had trying to get to Redlands using a car belonging to my friend's brother. This was wartime and tires were impossible to get so we had to just keep patching the same tire.

To make a long story short, we abandoned the car in Redlands and did make it to the cabin with eleven of us in one of the boy's cars that belonged to his dad.

Here is a picture of my girlfriends from work and the boys we met in Redlands. Mom took the picture. Imagine all of us in one car!

Marilyn, Terry, Kris, Evy and Ginny

Going home Sunday night, we dropped the boys off at the campus and returned his dad's car to him in Ontario. When we got to Ontario, Mom called the bus station and found there was a bus leaving for Los Angeles in 8 minutes.

When the bus got there, the driver said they only had room for six. Mom told him that we needed those six seats as we had had seven flat tires and had to get to Los Angeles as we girls had to go to work Monday morning. He said, anyone who had 7 tires didn't need a bus and Mom said the flats were all on the same tire.

Besides all our stuff, Mom had a kettle of beans, six eggs and a pound of butter and a loaf of bread in her lap. We got home at 10:30 p.m. and Mom wrote in the book, "I wouldn't have missed the excitement for anything!"

Two memories that stick in my mind involved the many many trips to our cabin driving through miles and miles of orange groves. In my early days, California was orange groves from San Diego to Santa Barbara. Along the route, there was an occasional Orange Julius Stand. We would stop and enjoy this delicious drink. Checking on Google, I discovered that Orange Julius was bought by Dairy Queen.

My mom loved to put orange blossoms in her tea. Not paying any attention to my dad's warning that she would be arrested, she would sneak into a grove and pick some orange blossoms on the way to the cabin.

All those miles and miles of orange groves from San Diego to Santa Barbara disappeared in my lifetime to become miles and miles of housing developments. Our track house in the 1950's was built in what had been a lemon grove. At the end of one block, there was still a small lemon grove that hadn't been eaten up. My boys would sneak in there and pick lemons and set up a lemonade stand on the curb…. always trying to make enough money to go to Disneyland.

The top edge of our tract was a nursery. The boys would climb over the fence and take plants that had been discarded (they said) and set up a stand on the street. The friendly neighbors would buy these half-dead plants.

As a kid, I was always complaining to my mom that I didn't have anybody to play with. My kids never had that problem. I counted 95 children on our block in Sierra Madre. Granted, it was a long block. The Walkers across the street had nine children. Everybody else had three to five.

My Mom always called me Baby. She would yell "Baby, it is time for lunch!"

Finally, I said, "Mom, stop calling me Baby!"

She said, "What can I call you?"

"Virginia, that's my name!"

When I wanted to play with a friend, I would go to her house and call, "Anna" and she would come out and play with me. Not so, with my boys. Their friends would ring the doorbell. How many times I answered that doorbell, and a little kid would ask for one of my boys. Why didn't they just yell the name of who they wanted to play with? (I know, I ended this sentence with a preposition.)

Chapter 9

Pets

Pets were a large part of my young life and still are. I'm still at the beck and call of my two cats, Sheba and Mooney. My son Tony said God created cats so we could pet lions.

As a young person, I had quite a variety of pets. A horny toad, rabbits, a jar of caterpillars I had collected, a dog named Cubby, and a chameleon named Ignatz. Ignatz lived in the windowsill in the breakfast room. I lost him once for days until I remembered I put him on a dark brown lampshade that he matched. I could hold him on my hand outside and he would catch flies. Sadly, my dad accidentally shut the window on him one day.

One Easter my folks gave me a baby duck I named Oscar. He was the best pet. My mom liked him because he would catch insects on her plants in the back yard. One horrible day, a dog caught and killed him.

Our neighbors would go fishing on the pier in Long Beach on the weekends. A cat they named Pete used to hang around them hoping they would give him a fish. One day, my neighbor decided to bring the cat home and gave him to me. If I wanted Pete to come home in a hurry, I would just yell "Fish, Pete!" Some months later, Pete gave birth to a bunch of kittens. That same month, Readers Digest had a cartoon with an old lady staring at her cat with a batch of kittens and saying, "Why, Pete!!!"

My cat, Wooley Bear, lived with us until after I was married and lived in the little house behind my mom's house. Jimmy was driving home from the restaurant where he worked late at night and ran over Wooley Bear who was sleeping in the driveway. My Mom and I were weeping and Jimmy said, "She was 20 years old!" I said, "You wouldn't run over your grandmother just because she was 100 years old!"

Jimmy and I received a wedding gift of a glass bowl shaped like a fish. We decided we needed a goldfish for this bowl. One day Jimmy noticed a growth on the fish's eye, and he operated on it. Would you believe, it survived the operation! I can't remember the name of that fish; it was only 86 years ago.

My son, John, outdid me in the pet department. He collected lizards, snakes, Jose the parakeet, guppies and worst of all, a monkey named Mickey.

I was amazed one day when John and I were standing on the balcony of his apartment, and he made a funny noise with his throat and a wild bird came and lighted on his hand. We always called him Nature Boy.

Chapter 10

Movies

Long Beach had a theater within a short driving distance of our house. We went almost every Friday night. It was 15 cents for adults and 10 cents for children for a double feature movie and a cartoon or maybe an Our Gang Comedy plus the News of the World. Sometimes there would be a give-a-way of dishes. Each Friday night, one plate or cup and saucer would come with your admission ticket. Eventually, you could acquire the whole set.

I remember one Friday night when we left the theater, it was so foggy we could barely see. Mom hung out the car window keeping an eye on the curb as Dad drove slowly down the street. That is the problem with living near an ocean.

One of the bigger theaters had vaudeville acts between the double features. Mom was anxious to go one night because a famous opera singer, Madam Schumann-Heinck, was going to perform. Recently, I looked her up on Google and she really was very famous. Doing a little arithmetic, I find that she was 68 years old when I saw her.

That night, Dad and I enjoyed the comedy act between features. A man came on the stage pushing a lawn mower chasing a girl in a grass hula skirt.

Between the two feature films, there would be cartoons. Walt Disney first created cartoons in 1928. I always say that I am four years older than Mickey Mouse.

Popeye was another favorite cartoon with his silly girlfriend, Olive Oyl. These cartoons were silly, but good, clean fun. I am horrified by the cartoons being made today. They are mostly violence and explosions. How do my great grandchildren sleep after an evening of that?

Seeing Hedy Lamar at the Hollywood Canteen was a thrill for me. She was behind the counter serving sandwiches to the service men. She was the most beautiful person I had ever seen.

This was 1941 and I was seventeen. Because the World War was in full force, my teacher at Los Angeles City College told us that companies were now hiring at seventeen. I joined 124 other girls working for the Aluminum Company of America (ALCOA) at the sales office in downtown Los Angeles. I wrote orders for the C47 airplane parts.

Betty Davis had opened the Hollywood Canteen in a building she owned to serve enlisted men in all branches of the service. All the services had officers' clubs, but nothing for enlisted men. These men came from all over the United States on their way to be shipped out of Los Angeles harbor. Betty Davis asked our company if they could send some girls to dance with these service men. Wednesday nights were the night for eight of us ALCOA girls to serve.

Lena Horn's husband's band played for us. We would come home with black and blue legs as these service men came from all over the country — some good, some bad dancers! Shirley Temple danced with the boys and the actor Willian Lundigan washed dishes in the kitchen in his Marine Corps uniform. We girls made a lot of trips to the powder room so we could see him.

One night, Roy Rogers came right in the front door riding Trigger. He sang, and Trigger did some tricks. Betty Davis had planned a big celebration to honor the millionth man to come through the door of the Canteen. They wanted some publicity pictures and asked my friend Marilyn and me to pose with a new starlet who needed some publicity. It was Ava Gardner.

I framed the certificate signed by Betty Davis. "In appreciation of your loyal service to the Hollywood Canteen." It now hangs on the wall above my computer.

In the old days, you could write to a movie star and ask for their picture. Just put their name on an envelope and write Hollywood, California. I had a collection of about ten pictures including my all-time favorite, Tyrone Power. I couldn't believe he married before he had a chance to meet me.

Among my pictures were Mae West, Jean Harlow, Simone Simone, Clark Gable, Tyrone Power and Loretta Young. When I was about 12 years old, a little girl was visiting us, and I thought I was getting too old to do childish things like collect movie star pictures, so I gave my collection to her. I did collect stamps and pennies which I also gave away when I thought I was too big for them.

Working in downtown Los Angeles, there was a theater a few blocks from our office. It was only 15 cents because the movies were old reruns. We would take our lunch bag and eat it at the theater probably watching a movie we had already seen. One movie we saw was Random. Harvest. I just saw it again on T.C.M.

When we lived in Sierra Madre, we had a little theater in town with a single aisle down the middle. In 1956, the movie *Invasion of the Body Snatchers* was filmed in our town. This was a horrifying movie with pods taking over bodies of the townspeople. Every year, the town celebrated on "pod" day with pods turning up in store windows and even on the mayor's chair.

Another crazy thing in town was a sculpture of a big spider in the park. The real spider was a violin spider, the size of a dime. Its venom kills in 15 minutes. Originally from Brazil, it made its way to the funeral home across the street from the park. It probably arrived in someone's luggage.

At ninety-nine years, my evenings are mostly spent watching Turner Classic Movies if there isn't a baseball, football or basketball game on TV.

I go to Guide once a week and record all the movies I would like to see. I check the actors, the year the movie was made, and if it is a three star. I might watch a two star if I like the actors. I find many of the silent movies made in the 1920's quite interesting. I watch anything with Mae West, Greta Garbo, Cher, Burt Lancaster, Tyrone Power, Barbara Stanwick, Lawrence Olivier, or Clark Gable. I thought Olivia DeHavilland was insipid, but she lived in Paris until she passed away at 105.

In the early days, the Hays Office had a set of rules and guidelines that Hollywood films were made to follow between the early 1930's and the late 1960's.

One of their crazy rules for films was married couples had to have a bedroom with twin beds. No swear words were allowed. When *Gone with The Wind* was produced, they made the one exception: Clark Gable could say at the end of the movie, "Frankly, Scarlet, I don't give a damn."

If the movie is made after 2000, I skip it because the language is usually full of the f word. The last time I went to a movie theater, the sound was so loud, I couldn't stand it. Now theaters are almost extinct. They tore down the only theater in Carrollton, but you can still see movies in the shopping center complex.

I have always had a policy not to turn the TV on before the six o'clock news (unless there is a sporting event). I pour my glass of wine and fix a dish of chips. After the phone call at five o'clock from one of my boys, I settle down for an evening of TV. Daytime hours are reserved for reading or writing. Of course, in the "old days," I was playing golf in the daytime hours. I really miss golf and often dream I'm playing in a tournament! I really did make two holes in one.

At 99, I do repeat myself a lot. So, if I have already told you about my trip to Warner Brothers Studio when I was sixteen, you can skip the next part.

I was a member of Job's daughters. To raise money for our organization, we sold doughnuts. The girl who sold the most doughnuts would win a trip to Warner Brothers

Studio because one of the girls' dad worked there. I sold the most to my teachers and friends and my poor Mom had to help me deliver them on a rainy night.

It was all worth it! At that time, the movie studios didn't want people to know how they faked everything. The girl's dad took me to the commissary for lunch as I stared at the movie stars sitting around us. The next table had five cowboys including Victor Jory.

After lunch, he let me peek into a studio filming Errol Flynn acting as a Navy doctor operating on somebody. I saw an old train and station that was used many times and a long street of houses with just the fronts of the buildings. If you have seen as many movies as I have, you recognize the bar rooms used over and over in Western movies. Also, I was told that you would never see a ceiling in a house in a movie. Check that out!

When you see people driving in a car, the car is standing still and the scenery, painted on sheets, is moving behind them. An old western street of false fronts had stunt men jumping off the roof. Cowboys were riding horses with painted backdrops of the desert behind them.

One trouble they had in the old days was filming a gigantic scene of hundreds of people in a historical movie and an airplane flying over. They would have to do the scene over. Nowadays, they could just cut the plane out.

The most remarkable thing I saw was the biggest sound stage in the world. Opening a door in this gigantic building, I peeked in to see mountains with telephone poles going over them, pouring rain and lightning striking the telephone wires. The movie was *Manpower* starring Edward G. Robinson, Marlene Dietrich, George Raft, Alan Hale and Frank McHugh. It was only recently that I saw the movie on TCM It was acquired from Warner Brothers Archive collection, thanks to Robert McCleary. Watching the storm scene, I realized how incredible that building was.

Chapter 11

Radio

The first crystal radio was invented in 1920. I don't remember having a radio until we moved to Long Beach in 1929. It stood on four legs. I would sit on the floor in front of it at five o'clock and listen to Little Orphan Annie.

The transistor radio was invented by Bell Laboratories in 1947. In the 1950's that enabled me to sit on a stool in the front yard and pull weeds while I listened to the Dodger games.

The Dodgers were playing the White Sox in the 1959 World Series. I was on my way to the hospital to deliver Tony, my fifth child. I took my transistor radio with me to the hospital and the doctors and nurses listened to the game while I was delivering.

Soap Operas on radio were another time pass-awayer. I would listen to them while I folded mountains of diapers. There were no throwaway diapers in my day. We had to soak cloth diapers in a bucket of water with vinegar to keep the smell down until they were washed.

The soap opera Days of Our Lives is still broadcasting on the radio according to a friend who has been listening to it since it started 58 years ago. She would hurry home from golf not to miss it. Actually, my dad got hooked on it when he was in his 80's and that was well over 20 years ago.

The good thing about radio is you can listen while you are doing something else, driving a car or cleaning house. When I was in junior high school, we always ate dinner at the dining room table. If it was prize fight night, my dad and I would listen to the fight on the radio while we were eating. We always bet 50 cents on our pick of fighters. Imagine listening to a fight. "He punched him in the belly..."

One Christmas, we gave each of the boys a little radio to use as an alarm clock, a Dream Machine – Wake up to music tape/Dual alarm. That was about sixty years ago and believe it or not, I still have mine next to my bed. The clock lights up in the dark so I can see what time it is in the middle of the night. I will have to check to see if the boys still have their Dream Machine.

Nowadays, everything is made to breakdown sooner or later. A good example of that is nylon stockings. Originally stockings were made of silk. They were easy to snag and run. So, someone invented nylons that didn't run. The manufacturers soon realized that they weren't selling any more stockings because they didn't run and lasted and lasted! So, then they made them so they would run!

Chapter 12

Television

We had three kids before we got a television set in the 1950's. I insisted that we get a piano before a TV, as I was afraid we would never get the piano.

The first television set I saw was when I was attending a Spinster meeting at a friend's house. The Spinsters were a group of high school girls, and I was invited to be a member in my senior year (1941). The group continued on until after we moved to Georgia in 1990 and they all came for a visit with their husbands fifty-four years later!

The Spinster member, Connie, was so excited about her new TV which was about 12 by 14 inches in size. There was only one program on it and that was the Nuremberg trials charging the Nazi baddies of World War II so that is what we watched.

In the 1960's my in-laws bought a giant size TV, even bigger than the one I have at present. We were all invited to watch the Rose Bowl Parade and the Rose Bowl game.

My son, Jim, went by the name Bernie (his middle name) before he went to school. I had called Sheriff John of *Sheriff John's Lunch Brigade*, to tell him it was Bernie's 5th birthday. When the program came on our TV, Bernie came running in the kitchen to tell me that there is another Bernie out there. I had to convince him that the Sheriff was singing to him.

The boys could watch TV until 8 o'clock if they weren't out playing in the neighborhood, and then Dad watched the news. The TV channels shut down at 12 midnight.

Advertising dates back to the Egyptians, but TV advertising has reached an all-time annoyance level. On July 1, 1941, the first commercial was aired by WNBT in New York before a Brooklyn Dodgers ball game. The black and white commercial was a watch head on the map of North America and a voice that said, "America runs on Bulova time."

Many of today's commercials on TV are sickening to watch—especially the ads for weight loss. Promoting pills for every health problem should be banned. Your doctor should make this decision for you. The My Pillow ad makes it almost impossible to watch the 6 o'clock news.

Today, TV runs 24 hours and advertising is constant and horribly annoying. I record the baseball, football and basketball games and watch them when I want to. Then I can advance forward and skip the advertising. TCM is relatively free of advertising and you can fast forward through their wine commercials.

Chapter 13

Ballroom Dancing

As far back as I can remember, my folks went to dances at Betty's Barn almost every Saturday night. It was somewhere out in the country—out of Los Angeles. When I was little, I would just sleep on a couch while my folks danced. When I was old enough, I started dancing and learned to do all the different kinds of dance steps: waltz, tango, foxtrot, rumba, Viennese Waltz and square dancing. Sometimes, my folks would take my girlfriends, too.

My mom told the funny story when she was young, she was dancing a square dance on the second floor of a building. One of the men in the 8-man circle had only one arm and she was afraid that going around to grab for his arm, she would fly out the second story window.

Dancing goes way back in history starting with belly dancing that ended up with the burlesque queens doing the bumps. Jimmy's family coming from Macedonia and Slovenia brought their dances with them called the kola, similar to line dancing with the leader waving a handkerchief.

One night in Sierra Madre, our neighborhood celebrated New Year's Eve at a Greek restaurant in town. Playing a record of kola music, Jimmy got up and started waving his handkerchief and we all followed him out the door and down the street. The owner thought we were leaving without paying our bill, but Jimmy danced us all back into the restaurant.

Los Angeles had "halls" for the different European countries where their mutual immigrants would meet and dance their particular style. Jimmy took me to the Macedonian hall, and I learned how to do the kola. Our wedding reception was held in the Swedish Hall. My mom hired the band from Betty's Barn and Mimi hired their Macedonian band. It was probably the only wedding where there was no intermission as the bands took turns playing. Grandpa Jim's restaurant served the food.

In old movies, you sometimes see minuets and fancy ballroom dancing with people dressed in gorgeous costumes of the 1700 and 1800's.

In my high school years, it was swing and jitterbug. The school band played for us on Wednesday after school in the girl's gym. It was called a "hop". A popular silly song was "Three Little Fishies in an Itty Bitty Pool".

"Three Little Fishies in an Itty Bitty Pool. Swim said the Momma, swim if you can, and they swam and they swam right over the dam. Be Bop didam dam, wadam chew, Be Bop didam dam, wadam chew, and they swam and they swam right over the dam!"

This was also the time of the Big Bands: Harry James, Bob Crosby, Glenn Miller, Artie Shaw, Count Basie, Woody Herman, Benny Goodman, Tommy Dorsey, Jimmy Dorsey, and Duke Ellington. I can honestly say that I danced to all of these bands at the Palladium or the Cocoanut Grove Ballroom at the Ambassador Hotel, Pasadena Civic Auditorium, the Balboa Ballroom and Duke Ellington at the Cotton Club in Los Angeles.

Jimmy and I danced to Glen Miller at the Palladium when he played "In the Mood". The band would stop mid-song and we would keep dancing and then the band would start up again right on beat. It was so cool!

One night at the Palladium, (dancing to Tommy Dorsey's band), we realized everybody had stopped dancing and had gathered by the stage. There was this crooner holding the mike by his ear and singing "I'll Never Smile Again". They were enthralled by Frank Sinatra who became the big sensation.

This was the beginning of Jimmy's love affair with Frankie. He had all of his records and played them in the garage while cutting the boy's hair or getting them to clean out the garage or wash the cars. The boys really hated his favorite "I Did It My Way".

"Yes, Dad, we'll do it your way."

I asked my daughter-in-law Jessie to enter "In the Mood" on her cell phone and it played the song and I tried to dance hanging on to a doorknob. I really miss dancing. Do high schools have Senior Proms anymore?

Every city had a ballroom where these bands played. These were where my dates would take me to dance. Out on Catalina Island was the Casino Ballroom. It has 50-foot ceilings with five Tiffany-like chandeliers, an elevated stage, raised seating areas surrounding the wooden dance floor. The most romantic part was the sweeping veranda surrounding the ballroom with a 360-degree view of Avalon Bay and the beautiful harbor lights.

I can't tell you how romantic this was. When I was there, the band was Bob Crosby. To my great surprise, I put in Bob Crosby in the Google line and up came Bob Crosby playing in 1938 which was when I was dancing to him at the Casino Ballroom. Check this out and you can hear the band playing and everyone dancing, gals in high heel shoes!

I say "was" because it is still there but only being used for wedding receptions. By the way, Bob Crosby was Bing Crosby's brother.

It is hard to believe that there are no more ballrooms. What a shame! You young people are missing a lot. Below is a picture of us dancing on our 50th Anniversary at Johnny's Hideaway in Atlanta.

Chapter 14

Fashion

What female isn't interested in fashion? In my day, fashion was decided by a group in New York. It was changed each year so that to be in style, you must buy something new. It all started with the length of skirts after the full-length skirts, worn in the 1800's, were no longer being worn except for formal wear. That is one style that has never come back except for muumuus in Hawaii.

This group in New York also decided what colors were going to be in fashion. One year the color was maroon—a color that I detest. Orange is one of my favorites and those two really clash!

From the long skirts of the early 1900's and even centuries before that, the 1920's skirts shot up above the knee for the first time. And from then on, they changed almost every year so that it was expensive to stay in style. Watching old movies, I can almost tell what year the movie was made by the length of the women's skirts.

When I was getting married in 1947, my friends gave me a wedding shower. We were all wearing skirts above our knee and my cousin Jean, who was attending Berkely at the time, came in a skirt down to her ankle. We thought she was weird. But guess what? She was wearing the newest style.

What made this so terrible was because my mom had made me this beautiful trousseau with all the skirts just above the knee. Soon pregnant, I never wore those beautiful clothes again.

By the way, these same fashion designers decided what color our kitchen appliances were going to be. "How about avocado for next year?"

How did those women traveling in covered wagons across our country manage in those floor length dresses. Even in towns, roads were dirt and muddy when it rained. It took more than 2000 years for women to get smart and not wear floor length gowns.

That is one good thing about today; skirts can be any length and nobody cares. And not only skirts, women started wearing pants when

Kathryn Hepburn wore pants playing golf. And they can be any length!

Another good thing about today, corsets and girdles have gone by the wayside. Corsets were worn to create a tiny waist line. In the film *Gone with the Wind*, remember Scarlet being laced up by her Mammy?

Shortly after the United States' entry into World War I in 1917, the U.S. War Industries Board asked women to stop buying corsets to free up metal for war production. This step liberated some 28,000 tons of metal, enough to build two battleships (according to Google.).

Leg makeup in colors to match your tan skin took the place of stockings during the war. This was really messy as it rubbed off on everything, but we ALCOA girls all used that stuff.

Elasticized girdles replaced the corset. Originally, silk stockings were held up above the knee by an elastic garter. This came about when skirt length also came above the knee in the 1920's. In my generation, we attached the stockings to our girdle until they invented pantyhose which I wear today. I think girdles have pretty much gone by the wayside.

An old wedding tradition was wearing something old, something, new, something borrowed, something blue. I wore my great aunt's garter (old) and my veil was borrowed from my friend Marlyn.

Another tradition from my day is the bride throws her wedding bouquet and the girl who catches it will be the next one married. The groom throws her garter to the men after ceremoniously removing it from the bride's leg.

Women's hats have disappeared with the exception of a sun hat, a golf visor or baseball hat. Gone are the days of beautiful hats trimmed in bird or ostrich feathers or flowers. Some styles in the 1800's were works of art you will only see in the movies.

Gloves were also a part of dressing up when I was young. Hats and gloves went together. What was crazy is that in Southern California where I grew up, gloves weren't needed to keep our hands warm. They were really just an appendage to complete our "look". We carried them along with our purse. I still have some leather gloves and cloth gloves that matched my outfits.

Another "must" in our closets were formal gowns for women and tuxedos for men. Our hospital auxiliary had a formal ball every year. Wessels was my favorite store in Sierra Madre and where I usually bought my formal gowns. One formal dance I wore gloves almost to my elbow. Also, one night I wore rhinestone strips on my eyelids. They were quite a hit! I have saved some of these formals for my granddaughters to see. Young people are missing "the dressing up" with no ballrooms anymore.

A whole different ball game are ski mittens, some with fingers and some with only a thumb. These aren't fashion; they were necessities in snowy weather. There was an old nursery rhyme from 1827: The Three Little Kittens

> Who lost their mittens
> And they began to cry....
> Oh, Mother dear,
> We sadly fear
> Our mittens we have lost.
> What? Lost your mittens,

You naughty kittens!
Then ye shall have no pie.
Mee-ow, mee-ow, mee-ow,
Then ye shall have no pie.

Another necessity in cold weather are earmuffs, but they hardly make a fashion statement.

Shoes have a history of their own. Leather shoes date back 7000 years, and the Romans made the first right and left shoe. In my ninety-nine years, shoes have had many different styles. In the 1950's I bought a pair of alligator platform shoes. They were very expensive and the platform design went out of style the next year!

My early fascination with the Orient started me wearing zoris which were sold in the little Japanese stores on the pike in Long Beach. The top was a velvet strip that came between my big toe and the next toe to keep it on. The bottom was woven grass protected by a sole of rubber. It was not unusual to see Goodrich tire printed on the sole as the Japanese were probably the first to recycle.

My mom used to take her visiting relatives and friends down to the harbor. We would see Japanese ships loading all our wrecked cars, tires and junk to be recycled into their war machine preparations.

I wore sling pumps all my life until my Doctor Simone Berard said to me one day, "I see you are still wearing falling down shoes!" Now I'm relegated to wearing flats, but I just can't throw away some of my fancy high heel shoes. I show them to my granddaughters along with my hats. Young women are still wearing the 4-inch-high stiletto heel.

Men wear zoris also, but they pretty much wear the same leather shoe tied with shoestrings even though shoes fastened with Velcro were invented in the 1980's. Unfortunately, when my boys were little, I had to tie their shoestrings until they learned how to do it. Tony wondered how many shoestrings I tied over the years and wanted me to figure out how many school lunches of peanut butter and jelly and baloney and cheese I prepared. That is depressing!

Men are still wearing boring clothes, with the exception of a few entertainers, but men and women both wear shorts—in public! Men do wear bright Hawaiian shirts.

When our country was founded, the men wore fancy lace trimmed clothes and even fancy wigs and knee-length pants. In several hundred years, that fashion has never come back except in England where the judges still wear wigs.

Just this week, the Congress had a big flap over wearing suits and ties to work. One Congressman wanted to wear sweatpants and sweatshirt. Thankfully this travesty didn't happen. Suits and ties prevailed.

When I was young, men always wore hats: Stetsons, Fedoras or cowboy hats and in summer, Panama straw hats. Today, if men wear a hat it is usually a baseball cap.

Wedding clothes are still pretty formal and those attending the wedding usually dress nicely.

All the sports have their own styles designed for comfort and protection. Court room lawyer attire is still suit and tie and the judges wear a robe. Even lady judges wear a robe.

A day I celebrated was when no-iron fabric was invented. I had spent hours at the ironing board ironing my boy's and my husband's shirts. Now, I don't know where my iron is. Good riddance!

Holey-kneed jeans were my nemesis. Luckily, they invented iron on patches when my boys were little. Now, girls are wearing holey-kneed jeans to be in fashion!

Chapter 15

Hairstyles and Makeup

Women and men both change their hair styles, but women seem to do it more often.

"In the old days" women always had long hair. My mother-in-law said she could sit on her hair. My mother never cut her hair, but it never got very long. She would get a "marcel" at the beauty shop which was done with a hot iron and made waves in her hair.

For centuries women had long hair and fastened it in a "bun" at the nap of their necks. When the "bob" came in style in the 1920's along with short skirts, bangs on her forehead and spit curls on her cheek were the "cat's meow".

I think the page boy was first worn by my generation although it probably came from young boys who were pages in courts. It was "the hairstyle" of the 1950's and usually worn with bangs. I still have bangs and a page boy seventy years later, not to say I didn't have a variety of hairstyles during those years. We wore up-do's, braids pulled across the top of our heads, ponytails, and pigtails with big hair bows when I was young. My little great-granddaughters wear big hair bows just like I wore when I was little.

I had straight hair and Mom had some cloth things that she would wrap my hair around and make "Shirley Temple" curls. As I got older and someone had invented the permanent wave machine, I sat under that while my hair was curled on heated rollers. It would last for several months before I would have to get another permanent. They were torture!

Eventually, I learned how to roll my wet hair on rollers and let it dry curly. Beauty shops had big hair dryers you sat under, but the personal hairdryer used today hadn't been invented yet. I did my own hair in high school. It was long enough to do braids wrapped over my head if all else failed!

The use of the "rat" began in my early working years. This was a wad of something that you put under your bangs or under long hair with a snood to hold it together to make your "page boy" hair style fuller. A snood was like a hairnet.

I had a horrible experience when I was dancing with a Marine during the war at a Hollywood night club. His watch on his wrist around my neck, caught in my snood and we were entangled on the dance floor. Even funnier, when we Alcoa girls rode on the cable car in San Francisco, the wind blew my friend Kris' rat out of her hair, and it went flying in the wind. We laughed so hard at Kris' chagrin.

The "wiglet" appeared in the 1960's and I wore one on top of my hairdo especially when attending formal dances. Wigs are still doing a big business for women, especially those who have lost their hair from cancer treatments.

In Sierra Madre, Jimmy was making enough money that I could go to the beauty shop every couple of weeks. My hairdresser loved to experiment on me, and she did this horrible "ratting" job on my hair. That was combing it back against its grain and making it rough and fuller. That hairstyle actually saved my head when we were driving to Santa Barbara to my niece Nikki's wedding. We ran into a car on the freeway. No seatbelts yet, and my head broke the windshield, but the ratted hair gave my head some protection. I was a little dingy from the blow.

When I was around 40 years old, the gray hair started sneaking in. Making the bed together one morning, Jimmy said, "I wonder what it would be like sleeping with a blonde." It just happened that I had made a hair appointment in Los Angeles with my mother-in-law's hairdresser. Six hours later, I was a blonde.

Sitting in the bleachers at one of the boy's games, my neighbor, Tom Brown, sitting behind me, poked me and said, "Virginia, do old blondes have more fun?" I could have smacked him!

For years I bleached my hair until I realized that my hair had turned completely white. Now. I can "do" my own hair, but every four weeks my hairdresser, Morgan, whom I have been going to for forty years, comes to my house and cuts my hair and does my nails. She had retired and moved to just over the border in Alabama. She raises chickens and brings me a few dozen eggs every time she comes.

Makeup is part of a woman's existence: eye-brow pencil, mascara, lipstick, rouge, and foundation. Eye makeup and aromatic ointments were found in Egyptian tombs dating back to 3500 B.C.

Queen Victoria abhorred makeup and so in the 18th and 19th centuries, she made it a taboo, with only prostitutes and 'loose women' and actresses allowed to wear it. In Hollywood's Golden Age, Max Factor, a make-up artist, was known for creating makeup for the famous stars. Thus, his pancake makeup became the norm for all of us crazy women.

Reddening of lips was done in Egyptian times, but our use of lipstick truly began in 1915 when Maurice Levy invented the cylindrical tubes that housed lipstick in its familiar forms to us. And then Hollywood actresses in the 1930's spread the use of lipstick to all of us gullible women.

At 99, I only wear eyebrow pencil and lipstick and let the rest just hang out.

A little footnote here: Jimmy and I always made our bed together in the morning. One night we came in the bedroom and the bed had not been made. We looked at each other and Jimmy said: "Well, the world didn't come to an end!"

Hair style is important to women but what about men? Today, men are being as crazy as women about hair. Look at the baseball players who weave beads in their hair just like some women are doing. My boys thought the barbershop was the chamber of horrors but not quite as bad as the high barber chair set-up in our garage. Jimmy cut their hair and they hated it. All the while, he was playing his Frank Sinatra record: "I'll do it my way". The boys would say, "Yes, Dad, we know you will do it your way!"

Jimmy accidently shaved a dollar size spot on son Jim's head. Jim's teacher asked him who his barber was because he definitely didn't want to go there!

This was the time when long hair came in style for young boys because of the Beatles. One day, John refused to let Jimmy cut his hair, so Jimmy took him down to the barbershop. When they got there, John got out of the car and headed for the mountains. He didn't come home until dark.

All the fights that ensued because of long hair came to an end when Jimmy let his own hair grow long when we went to Europe to celebrate our twenty-fifth wedding anniversary in 1972.

Today, anything goes. Just checkout the hairdos of the baseball players. I'm not happy with this, especially the really long hair and beards on the men. I don't see how it can be comfortable playing ball in the heat of summer covered with long hair and a beard. And beads?

I still like butch haircuts on men and sideburns are kind of interesting. Men aren't as imaginative as women and thank goodness they don't wear eye makeup or lipstick yet.

Something men can do, but not women, is grow a mustache. To this day, Jim and Jac still grow mustaches. When we were living on San Gabriel Court, my husband and my neighbor Rosemary's husband, Bob, decided to grow mustaches. The whole time, Rosemary was having a fit because she didn't like mustaches.

One day having our cup of coffee together, she was still complaining about her husband's mustache. She couldn't believe it when I told her that Bob had shaved his off two weeks before!

Speaking of coffee, probably very few of my readers will remember the days of rationing in World War II. Each family received War Ration Book One in May 1942 for sugar rationing so stamps #19-28 were designated for one pound of coffee during a specified five-week period. When the time expired, so did the stamp. Coffee stamps could only be redeemed for family members over the age of fifteen. By February 1943, the ration was reduced to one pound every six weeks.

Besides sugar and coffee rationing, leather shoes were limited to one pair a year. My poor Dad didn't get any new shoes during the war as I always used his ration stamp. Fortunately for us young ladies, shoemakers started making shoes out of canvas which weren't rationed and a little stylish.

I can drink coffee until midnight. It has never kept me from sleeping. My Mom never drank coffee. She had a pot of tea with lemon for lunch and a big veggie salad every day of her life. Probably why she lived to 97.

Chapter 16

Automobiles

I was born along with the automobile. In the early days there were no traffic signals ... no traffic! Going for a Sunday drive became a common activity. We would drive to visit friends. When they weren't home, we would leave a note on their door that we were sorry we missed seeing them. Once, we came home and found a note on our door that our friends were sorry they missed seeing us.

Before traffic signals, often traffic would be backed up in all directions at the intersection. No one would give in. I remember my dad getting out and directing traffic so we could finally get moving again.

When traffic signals were first installed, they were a post at the corner with two flags that would drop down, Stop and Go, and a bell would ring when it was time to go again. Years later, when red, green and yellow lights replaced the flags and there was no bell sound, people would just sit there waiting for the bell sound until somebody would honk.

The early cars did not have turn signals. The driver stuck his arm out the door window, straight out for a left turn and arm bent up for a right turn, rain or shine! Bicycle riders still do that.

As the number of models of cars increased, it became a fun thing to recognize the different makes and models. As a kid, I prided myself on recognizing most of them (Ford, Chevrolet, Packard, Oldsmobile, Chrysler, Cadillac.). To me, nowadays, they all look alike!

I was shocked to see a Chevrolet advertised for $33,400 on TV. My Dad bought a new Chevrolet for $600 in 1933. But then again, bread was 5 cents a loaf and 8 cents if it was sliced. In 1930 gas was 17 cents a gallon.

My first trip to Europe, I was riding in a taxi in Rome to get my hair and nails done. A fantastic looking car went by us, and I said "Wow!" The cabby, with a big smile on his face, said, "Lamborghini!"

Over the years, Jimmy and I had many cars, mostly second hand from his folks when they purchased a new one. However, an early one that we purchased was a new 1947 Hudson Hornet. It was so plush, it had everything: a heater, a radio, armrests, and the first seats made with foam.

Two years later, we had just made the last payment. Jimmy was driving on a side street on his way to the University of Southern California. A truck backed out and took out the passenger side of the car. The driver jumped out and took all responsibility for the accident.

Later, when the insurance company took the case to trial, the driver denied the whole thing. This made Jimmy so mad, he changed his major from accounting to law.

I thought Jimmy would get our car repaired, but he said it had structural damage and he brought home a Ford. It was called the Sally Rand model. Sally Rand was a famous fan dancer in Chicago who wore nothing on stage but her fans which she could manipulate beautifully.

That was what our Ford had—nothing! No armrests, no heater, no radio and hard seats probably made from horsehair. Even worse, it was black!

Many cars later, all picked out by Jimmy (who liked to surprise me), I finally bought my first car, a pearl white 2000 Cadillac Deville. I was a widow and seventy-six years old. I didn't know it had a GPS system until my son, Jac, was driving it and he accidentally pushed a button above the mirror and a lady's voice said: "How may I help you?" We all jumped at this stranger in the car.

I drove this beauty until I was ninety-one and brushed a curb turning a corner and decided I shouldn't be driving anymore.

My granddaughter Mary's husband, Aaron, is a car collector who inherited many old cars that Mary's grandfather had collected in his barn in Jasper, Georgia. Grandfather Donald had a 1930 Ford with a rumble seat. In my high school years, we would go to football games riding in rumble seats or in "turtle backs."

Granddaughter Natalie in the rumble seat.

My high school graduation night after our dinner at the Biltmore Hotel, my boyfriend and I rode in a rumble seat all the way to Balboa and back. Arriving home at breakfast time, my dad was so mad at me, he wouldn't even speak to me. It was all very innocent.

An example of our innocence, at the dinner at our table for ten, everyone ordered milk except me who ordered hot tea. You should have seen the looks I got. Alcohol didn't cross our minds.

Granddaughter Camila saying goodbye as Aaron takes me for a ride.
(Note 1930 license plate)

Check the white sidewall tires and the running board ,.. something we could use on all of today's cars to make it easier for people my age to get in and out of a car.

It is frightening to me that cars and trucks are now capable of driving themselves. Besides having GPS to guide you to your destination, the car warns you if you are going across the lane line and if someone or something is behind you, don't back up! Those are good things.

No one needs to know how to read a map anymore. Too bad. I always loved planning and tracking a trip on the map. Maps used to be available at every gas station. Then we were only able to get a map at the Automobile Club.

I still have a file drawer full of old maps from driving trips. My main purpose was to avoid freeways or interstates as they call them in Georgia. They are so boring besides being jammed with trucks. Give me a nice country road through little towns.

Bob and I drove all the way from Georgia to Miami without going on an interstate and enjoyed all the little towns and scenery along the way. I know a great way to drive to Chattanooga sans interstate on a four-lane divided highway without all the trucks.

On our road trips, Bob and I would stay at Bed and Breakfasts along the way. So much more fun than staying at hotels and the breakfasts are always special plus you meet interesting people, the hosts and other guests. We did the same thing in Europe, and even in India, seeking out small hotels or bed and breakfast accommodations.

To pass the time away, riding in a car, we played several different games. The Alphabet Game involved starting with A and finding a road sign or a sign on a building or billboard starting with A and then with B and so on. It used to be a challenge to see if we could find the whole alphabet before we reached our cabin in three hours.

Remember Hangman, a game we played in the car, and Tony and Jessie and I would play it in restaurants waiting to be served. Another old one that I still play was making a word out of the letters on the license plate of a car in front of us at a stoplight.

My boyfriend, Bob, had his own car games. One was being the first to find a white horse or a cemetery. Chances of me finding a white horse in California was pretty minimal, but I guess his home state Ohio had horses.

On long car trips, our kids would get so antsy. We were driving in northern California through miles and miles of wheat fields. Instead of asking, "Are we there yet?" little 5-year-old John said, "When are we going to stop going around the same block?"

We were heading for Lake Tahoe. When we got there, John walked into the lake, reached down and caught a little fish.

To close this chapter, my daughter-in-law Jessica, who works at Walmart, was asked by a customer, "I'm looking for an Atlas?" Is anyone printing Atlases anymore? What a shame! Fortunately, my son Jim gave me Rand McNally's the international atlas published in 1974. (For some reason, they didn't capitalize the title.)

Another friend who volunteers at a used book place told me that they are no longer accepting sets of encyclopedias. In my youth, almost every family had a set of encyclopedias to help the kids with their homework. Now they have their smartphones and Alexa to answer any questions.

Alexa is almost human as she asks me if I want to watch something or listen to the news. Sometimes she is so talkative, I have to ask her to be quiet.

Chapter 17

Airplanes

Airplanes were invented before I was born, but not much before! My Uncle Art flew a Jenny in France in World War I. After the war, men flew Jennys around the United States giving people rides for a few dollars. My mom and Aunt Nellie paid for a ride in a Jenny in South Dakota when they were teenagers. Standing next to the plane, when the propeller began whirling, it blew their skirts up over their heads, much to their embarrassment.

The year I was born, 1924, three U.S. Army planes landed in Seattle, having completed the first round-the-world trip by air in 175 days. My friend, Bob, and I flew around the world in 48 days in 2012 landing in many countries and staying a week or so in each country.

When my husband joined the Navy Air Force in World War II, his mother told him not to fly too high or too fast. Wrong! He was flying a C47 and landing on aircraft carriers.

By 1947, when Jimmy and I flew to Mexico City on our honeymoon, it took eight hours from Los Angeles. I was fascinated with looking down on the beautiful cloud formations.

Airplanes got bigger and bigger. I flew in a three-story plane to India. Flying in First Class is very comfortable with seats that make beds and free food and drinks.

Jimmy wasn't happy until he and a neighbor in Sierra Madre bought a plane. That was my first experience in a small plane. One Sunday, he and I flew from El Monte airport to San Juan Capistrano. Getting aboard to fly back, I discovered that my door wouldn't lock. Jimmy took a ribbon that decorated my purse and tied the door shut. I never flew in that plane again.

I have to admit that we had many wonderful flights to ski resorts, and when we acquired a twin-engine plane, we flew to New Mexico. Forgive me if I am repeating myself with another flying story:

Our friend, Nick Argy, wanted to go flying with us, but every time Jimmy would call, his wife, Betty, would have some excuse.

Nick said, "Call some Sunday morning early before she can think of an excuse." So, the four of us took off for Catalina Island to have lunch. The runway is very short and just drops off at the end.

On the way back, Nick wanted Jimmy to land at an airport that had some old planes exhibited. As we were coming in for a landing, our radio said, "Check fire on left wing." Betty and I froze! Actually, it was a fire on the ground that they wanted us to check out.

You will have to read my book, "Grossly Outnumbered" to read about Jimmy building an airplane in our garage in Apple Valley and flying it to Georgia.

A friend of Jimmy's had a little old plane with open cockpits. He took me up in it and I sat behind him. He told me to keep my mouth closed so bugs didn't fly in!

In my lifetime, air travel has become faster and faster. Eight-hour flights are now about four hours. And to top it off, now a flying car has been proven successful. I don't plan on trying that out any time soon.

Flying to the moon happened in my lifetime and maybe a human will land on Mars soon. In my early days, it was thought that it would take three generations living in a capsule to land on the moon. Wrong!

Our first plane ... the one with the door tied closed with a ribbon

Chapter 18

Space

Space travel was talked about when I was young. We haven't made it to Mars yet, but the moon is easy. Our neighbor in Sierra Madre worked at JPL (Jet Propulsion Laboratory) where much of the work was done to prepare for space travel. He helped our son, Jon, and his own son build a rocket. They took it out to the Palm Springs desert and flew it and actually retrieved it.

Soon, if you have enough money, you, too, can fly to the moon.

Edwards Air Force Base was near our house in Apple Valley. Chuck Yaeger, who broke the sound barrier, lived across the street. Jimmy and his friends owned together all kinds of airplanes including an acrobatic one that were kept in a hangar at the Apple Valley airport.

I took flying lessons there and my instructor loved to scare me to death. He turned off the engine midflight and asked me, "Where are you going to land?

I said, "There is a dry lake up ahead."

He said," You won't make it that far."

So, I landed in the desert near the highway. Then he said, "You had better take off or people will think we are in trouble." I never got my license because I refused to solo.

Jimmy built the Glassair plane below in our garage and on my birthday morning he said "I think I'll fly the little bird today." I panicked and begged him not to fly it for the first time on my birthday.

When he came home, he was grinning from ear to ear. I said, "You flew it didn't you?" He said he was just going to go down the runway and it just took off!

Jimmy flew the little bird to Georgia and his friend followed in our twin-engine Cessna. When Jimmy had to have a pacemaker, he couldn't fly anymore without a licensed pilot with him but that was easy because some Delta pilots also had planes there.

His last day on earth, he played golf in the morning. In the afternoon, he drove into town to get some slats to finish the deck and got a speeding ticket on the way back. He finished the project and chopped some wood. That night he said, "There is nothing good on TV tonight so I 'll build a fire and we can read." He passed away in his sleep after midnight on November 18, 1999. He was 75 years old.

Chapter 19

Smartphones and AI

So, call me old-fashioned or maybe stubborn is the right word. I just finished writing a book called *Very Truly Yours*, bemoaning the fact that no one is writing letters anymore. Instead of writing a letter, people just text on the smartphone. But you can't save a text message for a lifetime like you can a letter in your hand, to be read over and over again in your twilight years.

And I haven't even mentioned zoom calling on the computer where an unlimited number of people can be communicating and seen at the same time, the world over!

New inventions are flooding the market and the newest is AI—Artificial Intelligence. Now that is frightening! My granddaughter, Camila, who just turned 21 told me that AI can show you how your children will look. She said it was uncanny when she saw how her children will look! Her "little me" was "interesting and scary."

My granddaughter Brielle has just launched an AI program for Walmart and Jac tells me that robots will be having babies even if women don't.

Chapter 20

Shopping

My first recollection of shopping was my mother taking me to J.C. Penny's Department Store in Santa Ana. I was fascinated with the way a person paid for their purchases. The clerk would take the customer's money and put it in a metal container that she fastened to a wire cable that shot the money up to the mezzanine where the store's offices were located. The change would come flying down in the little container.

Trying on shoes meant the salesman would put my foot in the shoe and turn on the fluoroscope showing the bones of your foot and the outline of the shoe. If there is room for your foot to grow and not be too tight could be seen by me, the clerk and parent. It wasn't long before this was discontinued as using X-ray was obviously a dangerous idea.

My mother insisted I wear oxford shoes. I hated them as they looked like boy's shoes with shoelaces. I wanted Mary Janes with straps instead of laces. Those names are still attached to shoes.

Shoes without laces or straps are called pumps. The heel can be any height. Pumps come in strapless, no strap, t-strap, ankle strap, sling-back, peep toe and wedges. Heels can be flats, high, or stiletto. Lots to choose from today.

Since my mother made all my clothes, I didn't go shopping for clothes until I was married. My favorite store in Los Angeles was Bullock's Wilshire. When you drove in the parking lot, an attendant would park your car and bring it back to you when you finished shopping. My girlfriends and I would meet there for lunch in the fourth floor Tea Room. During lunch, a fashion show would be in progress. Then we would go to the hat department and try on hats. Oh, what fun we had!

Every town had separate hat stores and shoe stores for men and women. Also dress shops and men's clothing stores. Even our little town of Sierra Madre had a men's tailor shop where Jimmy had a suit made just for him. My favorite was Wessel's Dress Shop. At Christmas time, Wessel's had a cocktail hour for men where clothes were modeled in hopes they would buy them for their wives for Christmas.

Wessel's clothes were quite expensive. When they weren't having a sale, they put clothes that hadn't sold in a while in a closet. One of the sales-girls showed me this closet and I would look through these dresses first without Mr. Wessel knowing it. I would try them on whether the size was mine or not because I discovered the reason most hadn't sold was because their size was marked incorrectly.

Our hospital auxiliary had a formal ball every year to raise money for crippled children and we members would bump into each other at Wessel's to find the perfect gown for the ball.

Thank goodness fashion shows have not gone out of style. Our hospital auxiliary also put on a fashion show often. Most of the time we used the local dress shops, and our members were the models and we set up a runway and held it in the backyard of one of our members.

One year we put on a professional fashion show at the La Canada Country Club. The famous designer Mr. Blackwell provided his models. It was a Sunday afternoon, and we insisted our husband's come. They were in shock when they saw Mr. Blackwell arriving in a full-length mink coat.

Living in Apple Valley in the 1980's, our country club put on a fashion show of clothes made before 1950. I modeled my wedding gown my mother made in 1947. Jimmy accompanied me down the runway wearing his Naval uniform with its gold ensign stripe on the cuff. He was waiting in the club bar for the fashion show to begin when some army air force men came in. They said he was the oldest ensign they had ever seen with his white hair!

Walking down the raised runway, my stepfather, Les, took the following picture just as Jimmy grabbed me and kissed me.

One of the first Walmart type stores was Akron. They sold most everything including dishes and furniture at very cheap prices. We laughed when we bought a set of dishes and other things there, calling them Early Akron! It probably all came from China.

Dime stores were prevalent and satisfied a need for little stuff. Now the dime grew to a dollar with the country now dotted with dollar stores. The dollar is almost a thing of the past as the dollar stores are now charging $1.50 and more instead of a dollar.

Online shopping has practically ended store shopping. Everyone just shops on their cell phone. Trying on clothes was the best part of the fun of shopping. Thank goodness we still have a Belk's department store in Carrollton where I can shop for a dress or shoes or sheets or towels or jewelry and men and children have their own department.

Nowadays I pay for almost everything with a credit card along with everybody else. My first credit card was an American Express card I bought when I arrived in Atlanta on Delta in the 1990's. They were offering "Frequent

Flyer Miles" with purchases using the card. Since I loved to fly, it seemed like a good idea. Now I use it so I can transfer miles to my boys to come visit me!

Chapter 21

Grocery Shopping

In the 1930's, my mom went to South Dakota to help take care of her father who had cancer of the jaw from smoking cigars. I was in junior high school and completely unprepared for preparing dinner for my dad and Uncle Bud.

I went to the Safeway market a block from home and asked the meat man for three pork chops and then bagged three potatoes. The manager said the potatoes didn't weigh enough to charge me as most people bought a whole bag full. The next day I bought three lamb chops and the third day I asked for three beef chops. The butcher said he couldn't wait for my mom to come home and tell her about my misnomer.

Canned food had its beginning when Napoleon needed to send food to his troops. My mom canned food every year when the new crops came in. She also bought canned food in quantity when it was on sale. My dad would be so annoyed when we moved every couple of years, and he had to transport all her canned food. When she moved to Georgia in her 90's, she brought not only the canned food she had canned, but a crate of canned tuna she had bought on sale.

I am happy to say that my granddaughter, Mary, plants corn and peppers and string beans every year and cans them in Mason jars just like my mom did.

Frozen food was on the verge of being developed in the late 1930's starting with frozen orange juice. It wasn't long before whole dinners were frozen, and markets had to install big freezer sections.

In the old days, the grocer bagged your fruits and vegetables. At the old Safeway store in Long Beach, the grocer let my mom pick out her own vegetables and fruit. She was the only one allowed that privilege as the grocer usually just grabbed a mixture of good and bad fruit and vegies for the customer. Now, of course, everyone bags their own stuff. I guess the markets have a lot of food thrown out at the end of the day.

My Mom bought food for the week, but my mother-in-law went shopping every day at Ralph's Market. Each morning, she would ask my father-in-law for money. He always said, "What did you do with the twenty dollar bill I gave you yesterday?"

She said, "I put it between two slices of bread and ate it!"

I think Mimi shopped every day because that was the custom in Europe as they didn't have refrigeration when she was growing up and she had a car. My Mom walked to the market.

In Sierra Madre, I lived only two blocks from Robert's Market and had a charge account. I could send the boys for items, and they could just charge them. I'm still charging, but with a credit card, also invented in my lifetime!

Just yesterday I learned that Walmart has started a drone delivery service. Maybe the sky will be filled with drones as well as cars and airplanes in the near future. Someone will have to figure out how to direct this traffic in the air. I have no doubt it will happen in 2024.

Chapter 22

Appliances

In today's world we have a kitchen full of appliances. Most of them have been invented in my lifetime. I grew up with an ice box—not a refrigerator. Our house built in the late 1920's was pretty modern as the ice box was built into the wall. Most ice boxes were free standing and made of wood. The iceman was responsible for keeping ice in our icebox, driving around the town bringing big squares of ice that kept foods cold. He chopped it from a huge chunk, and he would give us kids chips of ice to suck on. My kids had the pleasure of catching the Good Humor man driving down our street for an ice cream cone if they had a dime.

By the 1930's, refrigerators had replaced the ice box. Do you remember ice trays that made ice cubes? Now my refrigerator spits out cold water or ice cubes and has a big freezer section.

With a family of seven, we purchased a big freezer we put in the garage. I would buy bread at the day-old bakery 20 loaves at a time and freeze it. Preparing sack lunches for the boys used a lot of bread.

Our milkman said that anyone who drank more milk than we did had their own cow! Our dog Sheba would go across the street and bring our neighbor's milk bottles to our house. I traveled on a cruise with this lady years later and asked her why she never complained about our dog. She said it was no problem. She would just send one of her boys over to get their bottles.

The Fuller Brush Company has been in business since 1906. Their salesmen sold their brushes door to door on our street. We also had the Helm's Bread truck go by as well as the Good Humor Man.

The kitchen stove has also gone through many changes in my lifetime. The stove I remember as a kid was powered by gas. It stood on four legs and the burners and oven were at waist height. You had to light the burners and oven with matches. I was scared to death of lighting the stove. Mom was sick with the flu and she wanted me to heat some soup. I just cried and she had to get up and do it herself. I have always had an electric stove.

Jimmy's cousin, Stephitza, from Croatia was visiting us in Apple Valley in the 1980's. We had bought our first microwave oven. She was fascinated and said, "You are cooking with your fingers!"

One appliance I wish I still had was a toaster-oven. It prepared two slices of toast that would pop up when done or you could warm a bun or make a grilled cheese sandwich in a drawer on the bottom. Jon kept it working until it finally bit the dust. I've never seen another one like it. Instead, I have a toaster oven and microwave as well as a built-in electric stove top and wall oven.

The old stove-top coffee percolator is still around, but I have an electric drip pot.

Automatic dish washers, garbage disposals and clothes washing machines and clothes dryers were all invented about the time I was married in 1947. My mother was still using a hand wringer washing machine. Her husband Les always helped her wring out the clothes and hang them outside. She thought it good for the clothes to hang outside and get the fresh air.

My favorite story about my mom was when she read in the paper that they were going to stop making wringer washing machines. She panicked!

She called a company in Hollywood and asked if they had a wringer washing machine in stock. They had one and she told them to hang on to it until she got there. They thought this was hilarious. They called the FOX television station and then the station called my mom and they asked if they could come out and film her wringing out her clothes. She said they would have to come on Monday morning before 9 o'clock or she would be all finished! We knew this was going to be broadcast on the Six O'clock News on Thanksgiving night, so we all gathered around the TV to watch my mom open the program introducing her as the very modern woman playing her drum set Les had given her for her birthday and then demonstrating how she and Les washed clothes.

When Mom moved to Georgia in 1990, she brought that old wringer washing machine with her even though she had an automatic washer and dryer. She stored it in her garage, just in case.

Because my husband's mother made him help hang the laundry on the clothesline, he bought me an automatic clothes dryer before I had an automatic washing machine.

One thing I learned early on was to always empty pockets before putting clothes in the washing machine. My son Jon's pants pockets always held worms, snakes, seeds, leaves and other things I didn't recognize.

I loved my Selectric typewriter and then the computer took over. I guess the best thing about that is the original keyboard I learned in junior high school has never changed.

An amazing development in my lifetime is the remote controller. I can turn on the television without getting up from my chair as well as change channels. I can record movies for future viewing. I try to have a few old goodies saved for my sons to see when they visit.

Another great invention in my lifetime is the sliding glass door. Perhaps my love of these doors relates to my intrigue with Japanese architecture.

As a docent at the Asian Art Museum in Pasadena, my required report was on Japanese architecture. The fusuma sliding door between rooms and to exit onto a deck gave me the idea to build a deck (Japanese engawa) across the back of our house in Sierra Madre. I installed sliding glass doors in all the rooms all across the back of the house to view the pool. When we moved to Georgia, I was dismayed to find that all the houses here had double hung windows. My real estate lady asked me, "What other kinds are there?"

The first thing I did was change all the windows on the back of our house to sliding glass doors so we could get a wide-open view of the lake. This also makes it easy for me to let the cats in and out as I can slide open the glass door from my chair.

Vacuum cleaners were invented in my lifetime. I remember vacuum cleaner salesmen going from door to door selling vacuum cleaners. The broom and the mop still do kitchen duty. Some of the annoying salesmen that drove me crazy in my early married years were vacuum cleaner, insurance and encyclopedia salesmen.

When I had my first baby, these salesmen could get a list of new mothers' addresses and pounce on them. I finally put up a big sign on the front door: If a salesman rings this doorbell, it will be MURDER.

The phonograph was invented in 1870 by Thomas Edison. My mother-in-law had records of the famous opera singer Caruso. When I was in high school, many of my friends had a record player and collected records. I didn't. When we moved into the Carter Avenue house in Sierra Madre, the former owner, Mrs. Paul d'Orr, left a 1926 combination record player and radio with storage for her many records. She could even make recordings on it of her friends singing. Incorporated in the design were places for her collection of vinyl records. I still have this "contraption."

Jimmy and I did have a record player and Jimmy began bringing records home. He had opened a restaurant next to the Capitol Record Building in Hollywood. A regular customer was the composer, Alfred Newman. From the 1930's to 1960's Newman composed music for 20th Century Fox Movie Studio. He received 45 nominations for Oscar awards for his movie soundtracks. Mr. Newman would bring Jimmy records of these movie soundtracks. I have that whole collection.

In my "middle age," I started collecting record albums of my favorite singers. Favorites are Edith Piaf singing in French and Barbara Streisand singing those soft high notes.

Now people plug in their ear an MP3 Player and go ride a bike or take a morning run while they listen to music.

Chapter 23

Games

I wonder what games we played as children are children playing today? Remember hopscotch? Ring around the Rosie? Did anyone ever ask you to play 52 Pickup Sticks? How about Dodge Ball? Hide and Go Seek? "It" would cover his eyes and count to 100 while everyone would hide from him.

The games we played as children have changed over the years but some such as Blindman Bluff, Musical Chairs and Pin the Tail on the Donkey are still being played at children's parties.

Games I played as a youngster: Hide and Go Seek and Ring Around the Rosie, "a pocket full of posies, all fall down!" We played Kick the Can, Marco Polo, and Blind Man's Bluff. We drew hopscotch on the sidewalk with chalk. We chanted "Fee Fi Fo Fum, I smell the blood of an Englishman."

Playing Blind Man's Bluff, shouting "Olly olly oxen free" meant it was safe to come out into the open without losing the game.

The neighborhood kids made up a game. In the Poolman's front yard, they made a circle with a hose on the grass, and everybody got in the circle. The idea was to bump everybody out of the circle using their butts. When Mr. Poolman came home, he insisted on playing. Unfortunately, his butt was about the level of the kid's heads and it was big!

Mr. Poolman was very organized. He hung all his tools on the wall in his garage and outlined each one. It wasn't long before just the outline drawing was there. The kids had lost all the tools in the ivy planted in many yards, or in a vacant lot building forts.

I can't leave Bob Poolman without another story. He was a professor at Cal. Tech. Their students were notorious for playing jokes on their professors. One time, when a professor was out of town, his students built a brick wall so when he opened his office door, it was solid bricks.

Remember when college students did card stunts at the football games? Every student had a card with a big letter of the alphabet on it. When I was going to U.S.C., my friends and I always sat in the card section. One game day, Tech students had gotten hold of our cards and when they came up, it spelled Cal Tech instead of USC.

Knowing this, Jimmy and I were still unprepared for Bob's ingenuity. We were gone on vacation and had told the neighbors they could use our pool. That Friday night before we got home, they had a party in our back yard. I'm sure it was Bob's idea when they gathered all the newspapers from the neighborhood, crumpled them and filled our entire bedroom, floor to ceiling.

When I went down the hall, there was a sign on our bedroom door saying, "Smile, you are on Candid Camera." I opened the door and all I saw was crumpled newspapers. What really made me mad, is I had just put up new wallpaper.

I stormed out of the house and yelled from my front porch, "Bob Poolman, you did this!" Of course, he never admitted it. Jimmy and I thought for months trying to come up with something to get even. Jimmy was waiting for them to go somewhere, and he was going to bury two stakes on either side of their driveway and hang a chain across so they couldn't get in when they got home. They were afraid to leave, and they didn't!

On our street (San Gabriel Court) my sons played Ditch'em, Mother May I? Simon Says, and Congo. Marco Polo was in the swimming pool.

Every year they had a carnival in our back yard. Our neighbor Mrs. Holly was the fortune teller with a turban on her head and a glass ball to read the fortune. They raised money to go to Disneyland.

My son, Tony, was a game person. He loved to play games, but he also created games. He designed a card game with all the cards pictures of the presidents of the United States. When we started to play Scrabble, he created many new ways to play. First of all, instead of seven letters, we played with twelve making long words possible. Most importantly, we could play off of words in a single turn, as many words as you can make off of the original word. When the four red triple point corners are covered or the numbers left in the bag are less than 10, you can build on top up to three to create new words. Playing this way makes the original game seem very boring. Tom and I have a game almost every weekend and Jessie and I play.

Jessie taught me to play Mah Jong, the Hong Kong way. She told me that different countries play the game differently. She also taught Tony and my granddaughter, Camila.

My folks played auction bridge, but I learned to play contract bridge and still play once a week with my friends.

When my boys and I get together, we like to play Hearts. When we took a cruise to Cuba, we played every evening at 5 o'clock with our glass of wine in hand. I won every game! Knowing bridge helps with hearts.

Chapter 24

Computers

When Number Two Son, Jon, competed in and won the Science Fair in Junior High School (1960's), he used electro-mechanical relays to create a logic surface that allowed you to play Tic Tac Toe against the computer, but you could never win.

His early interest was in growing things, especially orchids which took him to the jungles of Central and South America and his graduate degree in biology.

The computer was the stronger pull, and his eventual career became setting up paperless systems in banks and public buildings from San Francisco to New York.

Number Five Son, Tony, was interested in video, and he was filming from an airplane over Pasadena. The man who hired him paid him with two computers (1980's). He sold one to me and then taught me how to use it.

Now I check my e-mail every morning and love keeping in touch with friends and family. You are reading just one more book prepared on my computer.

The computer has probably been one of the most important inventions in my lifetime. It keeps our far-flung family together and with the latest addition of Zoom calling, it has brought the world together face to face. The smartphone is really just a computer in your hand.

Chapter 25

Sports

Sports are still an important part of my life even though now I'm participating vicariously from my recliner. I root for the Atlanta Braves, the Falcons, Georgia Bulldogs, U.S.C. and the Atlanta Hawks. October 13, 2023, was an unlucky Friday the thirteenth! That weekend was a horrible loss by U.S.C. to Notre Dame 48-20, a big loss by the Atlanta Falcons to Washington Commanders 24-16 and the Braves were eliminated from the World Series playoffs! What a bummer!

Even more unbelievable, the Washington Commanders have the first black female assistant coach in NFL history, Jennifer King! Also, Alyssa Nakken is being interviewed for manager of the San Francisco Giants and she is expecting her first child!

I'm still a football fan of U.S.C. and root against U.C.L.A. and Notre Dame. That fan base dates back to my childhood. Our neighbor, Rocky Kemp, was the football coach at Wilson High School in Long Beach. He had played football at U.S.C. under the famous Howard Jones. He was able to give my dad an opportunity to sit on the bench with the U.S.C. players during a game one year. We had a football board game with a cloth felt football that we played.

My high school in Los Angeles was just a few blocks from the U.S.C. campus and we girls would walk to the Coliseum that was built in 1932 for the Olympics. It still has the torch at the top of the stands. It has always been the U.S.C. football field.

We could easily get tickets from students that weren't interested in the game and sit in the Trojan section and do the card stunts.

I was dying to go to U.S.C. but my folks couldn't afford the tuition, so I went to Los Angeles City College for $6 a semester. It wasn't until after I worked in Yosemite the summer of 1945 and saved enough money that I went one semester to U.S.C. taking Business Math, History of the World from 1450 to the Present, English Literature and Bacteriology.

My personal sports history was playing badminton with my dad on our neighbor's court, and I was ping pong champion in junior high school. My son, Jac, still won't admit I beat him at ping pong a few years ago.

When we were married, my husband's brother, Tom, was nine years younger and still in junior high school. He was always wanting me to stand in front of a mirror with him to see if he was taller than me yet. Actually, he grew to six feet three inches and was an all-American end on the U.S.C. football squad so my family went to four years of U.S.C. football games. Rain or shine and some-times so hot we would take wet towels to keep us cool.

Four of my sons played baseball, starting with Peewee and ending with the Colt League earning lots of trophies. Tom and Tony played Pop Warner football. In high school, Tom played in the Rose Bowl because that is where Pasadena High School team played their games. Jimmy and I were attending one of his games, me with movie camera in hand. All of a sudden, I realized everyone was looking up behind me. Tony, eleven years old, had climbed up the light tower. I couldn't look as Jimmy went up to coax him down. This added a few grey hairs.

Jac was a trophy winning baseball player, not interested in football until he saw Tom come home one day with his uniform covered in dirt. He said, "Maybe I would like to play football." I cringed at the thought of another dirty uniform to wash!

From nine years old, Jim swam every day for his whole life. That is a clean sport ... no uniform to wash! He still swims every morning in the ocean in Miami.

Besides badminton and ping pong, Jimmy and I were on a bowling team to raise money for Orthopedic Hospital. Jimmy didn't like the smoky atmosphere of the bowling alley, so we quit and took up golf and skiing. I skied until I was 84 when I fell and broke my shoulder on the slopes at Big Bear.

I played golf until I was 93 and am proud to say I had two holes in one. I really miss golf and often dream I'm playing in some tournament.

Chapter 26

Astrology and Travel

Marsha Johnson, the wife of a friend of my son Jim in the Peace Corps, sent me two quotations that I love and want to share:

"Do you have the patience to wait until your mud settles and the water is clear?"

"Can you remain unmoving until the right action arises by itself?"

I am also a reader of my fortune, checking out Virgo each day in the paper. One I saved from so long ago that it has yellowed.

VIRGO (AUG. 23-SEPT 22) You have style, and it shines through when you're in a new environment. You'll be a traveler but not a tourist. You'll experience a place for the first time and comfortably fit in there.

My mom read every travel book in our local library. But we never went anywhere after we built the cabin when I was eleven. Mom was married to my dad for twenty-five years and then she married Les Cross, and they were married twenty-five years before he passed away. They did travel the world together.

So, when Jimmy suggested getting a vacation house, I balked! Instead, we traveled, and I loved it! When I was expecting our fifth son, we went to Hawaii on the cruise ship Lurline, stayed for twenty-one days, and flew home (nine hours in 1959). My mom couldn't believe I was going when I was five months pregnant. I told her that I really needed a vacation and the doctor said I would be fine if I didn't ride a surfboard.

We hired a lady to take care of the boys and we thoroughly enjoyed our three weeks in Hawaii.

We went to Austria to ski Mutters in the 1970's and a fabulous trip to China visiting the Xian warriors in 1984. I can't describe my feeling standing on the edge of the underground tunnel looking down at a life-size army of 7,000 terracotta soldiers and horses in battle formations wending their way to the tomb of Emperor Qin Shi Huang two hundred years before Christ. Discovered in 1974 when a man was digging a well, they were still unearthing this phenomenon when we were there. What is truly amazing is that each clay warrior has a unique face.

On this trip, we sailed the Yangtze River starting from Wuhan. Yes, the notorious Wuhan where the Corona virus started. Ironically, I was sick in Wuhan and Jimmy called in a lady doctor. She said I was just getting old. (I was 50). Jimmy figured out that I was just dehydrated because I was reluctant to drink the water.

From Hong Kong, we flew to Taiwan and then to Singapore and Thailand where I rode my first elephant. If you know me, you know I am still nuts about elephants. Besides my elephant collection, I ride one every chance I get.

Jimmy and I cruised the Mediterranean taking in Greece and Turkey and trips to Croatia and Macedonia to see his mom's and dad's hometowns, Sisak and Bitola. We also visited the British Isles, France, Italy and Germany. Son Jim and I toured Italy, Jugoslavia, Greece India and Nepal where I rode an elephant. Son Tony and I sailed the Baltic Sea visiting

Sweden, Finland, Russia, Lithuania, Estonia and Denmark.

I was fortunate to meet Bob Fischer when Jimmy passed away. He liked to travel, and we did a train trip from Georgia to Idaho and back completing our goal of seeing all 50 states, cruised to Alaska, sailed the Danube, cruised the east coast of South America and up the Amazon River. We loved every minute we were in Africa. Then we flew around the world on Delta stopping in England, Scotland, Egypt, India, Korea, Bali, and Australia when I was 89 years old. I celebrated my 91st birthday on the Mekong River in Cambodia.

Who would trade a vacation house for all that? If you ask me where was my favorite place, I would have to say Nepal, Kenya, Zimbabwe, Bali and Thailand, but I enjoyed them all. As you might have guessed, I rode an elephant in each of these places!

Chapter 27

Jokes

Jokes have always fascinated me. As a kid, I. read the jokes on the bottom of the pages in Reader's Digest and would tell them to my teacher walking out to the playground. She told me I should spend more time studying school assignments.

When I was five years old, our neighbor came over and told my dad that this farmer had crossed a duck and a pheasant, but he didn't know what to call it. So, I piped up the obvious. My mother was furious and sent me to my bedroom and bawled the neighbor out.

I always wondered what I had said and didn't find out the meaning until I had been married a few years. Now, unfortunately, it is commonplace in the newer movies and even creeps in on TV once in a while.

One of my favorite jokes is the Big Mouth Frog joke. I told it on many occasions. On a cruise down the Danube, sitting at a table with six people from Australia, this lady told my big mouth frog joke! I guess jokes really get around!

My mom's second husband, Les, told this funny joke. Two cannibals were cooking a big pot of stew. One of them said, "I never did like my mother-in-law." The other cannibal said, "Well, just eat the noodles."

If you are a bridge player, the following joke will tickle your funny bone:

> A cleaning lady was applying for a new position. When asked why she left her last employment, she replied: "Yes sir, they paid good wages, but it was the most ridiculous place I ever worked. They played a game called bridge and last night a lot of folks were there. As I was about to bring in the refreshments, I heard a man say, "Lay down and let's see what you've got!" Another man said to the lady, "Take your hand off my trick." I pretty much dropped dead just then when a lady answered, "You jumped me twice when you didn't have the strength for one raise." Another man said, "I've got strength but no length." Another lady was talking about protecting her honor and

two other ladies were talking and one said, "Now it's time for me to play with your husband and you can play with mine." Well, I just got my hat and coat, as I was leaving, I hope to die if one of them didn't say, "Well, I guess we'll go home now. That was the last rubber."

Chapter 28

Health

In case you are wondering how I managed to live so long, I attribute it to an article I read many years ago about a man who stood on his head for a minute every time he sneezed. He said it kept him from catching a cold.

Not good at standing on my head, every time I sneeze, I stand up and bend over from the waist with my hands raised above my head and count to 160 fast. I don't know his theory, but mine is that this action brings the blood to my head carrying with it white corpuscles to fight any germ that might be lurking. Don't laugh! I've had one cold in the last 50 years.

Another suggestion involves eyes. I wore glasses in high school for distance because I couldn't read the numbers on the football players uniforms. I continued to wear these glasses driving until I was about 45 when I realized I could read signs better without them. And then I needed glasses for reading!

I don't remember when I started doing eye exercises, but they were incorporated into my daily morning exercises that start when I get out of bed. On arising, I look up, down, left, right, and then circle my eyeballs. It seems my eyes get better and better. Now I can see across the lake at the cars on the road behind the marina. I use dollar store reading glasses if I'm doing a lot of reading, but I don't need glasses to use the computer or watch TV.

Perhaps one reason for my longevity is I read Psalm 91 every morning before my prayers and Bible reading. When Covid broke out, Jessie copied Psalm 91 and posted it by our front door. I feel I am protected under God's angels' wings. "He will cover you with his feathers, and under His wings you will find refuge."

I wrote my first book in 1985: *Grossly Out-numbered* followed by four children's books *Granny with the Freckled Knees* and then *My Platinum Years*. A few years ago, I joined the Carrollton Writers Guild who meet once a month. We share our creations and ask for suggestions. Covid virus interrupted my attendance, but I do enjoy the group and plan to attend now that Covid is slowing down.

Because I've been typing all my life, my fingers are very agile. Part of my morning exercise routine is shaking my hands, clenching and unclenching my fists and separating my fingers individually.

Part of good health is taking care of your teeth. Part of my teeth heritage is from my mom. Admitted into the nursing home at 97, the nurse brought her a bowl of water to her bedside. Mom said, "What is that for?"

The nurse said, "It is for your teeth. My mom was adamant as she pointed out her teeth were her own.

Also, part of my good fortune is the fact that our town of Sierra Madre (Mountain Mother) had natural fluoride in the water coming down from that mountain. Consequently, my boys also have good teeth. Today, the Georgia water company adds fluoride to the water to help prevent teeth decay. Probably true all over the country.

Chapter 29

Women

A big change I have seen in my lifetime is the role of women in our world. I can't think of a single mother who worked outside the home when I was growing up. Possibly the change began when women were needed to work while the men went off to war in World War II. Even in our neighborhood when I was raising our kids in the 1960's, none of the women on our block worked outside the home.

I remember reading about how in communist Russia, all the women were put to work and the children put in childcare. That was the communist way. I think it is sad that today many mothers are choosing to work. In Chicago and even Atlanta and many other cities, mobs of children are raising havoc, robbing stores and shooting each other. Why are their parents not taking charge of their activities? They need to be taught right from wrong by their parents and it starts in early childhood.

It seems women will not be happy until there is a woman president. And if women stop having babies, our civilization will end.

Men and women were created differently for a reason. As they say: "Viva la difference!"

Chapter 30

Finale

My husband told me about his mother telling him, "I've been where you are going." One day driving along, Jimmy said to our son Jim, "I've been where you are going," and Jim said: "Maybe I'm going somewhere else."

Dear reader, when then meets now, wherever you are going, may it be fruitful and full of fun and love. Quoting from the Bible, Ecclesiastes 7:10: "Why were the old days better than these?"

They weren't better or worse, they were just different. Enjoy the difference!

Dedication

For those who remember and
those who are creating
their own memories

www.ingramcontent.com/pod-product-compliance
Lightning Source LLC
Chambersburg PA
CBHW070720240426
43673CB00003B/91